DK

Crafty
Science

Jane Bull

Design and Text Jane Bull
Editor Violet Peto
Designer Sadie Thomas
Science Editor Wendy Horobin
US Senior Editor Shannon Beatty
US Editor Margaret Parrish
Design Assistant Eleanor Bates
Photographer Andy Crawford
Producer, Pre-Production Dragana Puvacic
Producer John Casey
Jacket Designer Charlotte Bull
Jacket Coordinator Francesca Young
Managing Editor Penny Smith
Managing Art Editor Mabel Chan
Publisher Mary Ling
Art Director Jane Bull

First American Edition, 2018
Published in the United States by DK Publishing
345 Hudson Street, New York, New York 10014

A catalog record for this book
is available from the Library of Congress.
ISBN 978-1-4654-7768-2

DK books are available at special discounts when purchased
in bulk for sales promotions, premiums, fund-raising, or educational
use. For details, contact: DK Publishing Special Markets, 345 Hudson Street,
New York, New York 10014
SpecialSales@dk.com

Printed and bound in China

Material used in this book was first published in:
The Christmas Book (2002), The Magic Book (2002),
The Rainy Day Book (2003), The Gardening Book (2003),
The Cooking Book (2003), The Sunny Day Book (2004),
The Crafty Art Book (2004) The Baking Book (2005),
and Make It! (2008).

**A WORLD OF IDEAS:
SEE ALL THERE IS TO KNOW**

www.dk.com

Contents

!

Safety

Projects in this book may require adult
supervision. When you see the warning
circle, take extra care, and ask
an adult for help.

Sun clock

People have always used the sun to tell the time. Make yourself this useful clock for when you're out in the yard on a sunny day.

What's the time?
Impress your friends by being able to tell the time without looking at a watch. How do you do it? By using the sun.

What's the science?

Have you ever noticed how shadows grow longer or shorter depending on the time of day? **The shadow on your sun clock is affected by how high the sun is in the sky.** The shadow starts off long when the sun first comes over the horizon at dawn, gets shorter until noon, when the sun is overhead, and then grows long again as it drops below the horizon at sunset. Watch this happen on your sun clock.

You will need:

- Paper plate
- Stick or garden stake
- Terra-cotta plant pot
- Adhesive putty
- A watch
- Strips of paper

6

How to make a clock

Press the plate onto the putty.

Before you assemble your sun clock, decorate the plate, stick, and pot.

1 Make a hole in the center of the plate and push the stake through.

2 Now put the stake through the hole in the plant pot.

Put putty around the hole.

3 Make sure the plate is a tight fit around the stick.

Use the sunlight to set your clock

You will need a whole sunny day to set your clock so that you can read it the next day.

1 Place your clock in a sunny area.

2 The stick will cast a shadow across the plate. This is the sun telling you the time.

10 o'clock

12 o'clock

2 o'clock

3 Now look at your watch, and mark the shadow on each hour with a strip of paper. For example, at 10 o'clock mark the shadow, then continue until the sun goes down.

4 The next day, tell the time by seeing where the shadow falls!

Noon 12

Make the 12 o'clock strip look different to remind you where it is.

11 1 2
10   3
9   4
8   5
         6
         7

It's just past 3 o'clock.

Squeezed to meet you!

Thirst aid kit

This lemonade recipe makes just over one quart (1 liter). It may be tangy, so add sugar or extra water until it tastes good. The best thing to do is experiment.

Drink up

Your lemonade will only keep for two days in the fridge. Make sure you drink it quickly!

You will need:

- 3 lemons
- 1 quart (1 liter) water
- Sugar to taste

- Cutting board
- Sharp knife
- Measuring cup
- Blender
- Large cup or bowl
- Strainer
- Large spoon
- Funnel
- Bottle

Making lemonade

Scrub all the lemons well, since you will be using the whole fruit— even the rind!

1 Wash the lemons and remove the ends and seeds. Chop each into eight pieces.

2 Put the lemons into a blender and add some of the water.

! **Ask an adult** to help with the blender.

3 Blend until the mixture is smooth.

Ice pops

Place some fruit pops into an ice cube tray and simply fill with your lemonade. Put them into the freezer overnight, and you have ice-cold, fruity lemonade lollipops!

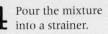

What's the science?

Put your **tongue** against the cut side of a lemon. That tangy, sharp taste is a shock, isn't it? Lemons are **sour** because they contain **citric acid**, which activates the **taste buds** on your tongue that detect sour flavors.

All citrus fruits contain citric acid, but some seem less sour because they contain more sugar. Try tasting grapefruit, limes, oranges, tangerines, and lemons together—which is the sweetest?

Remember to save some mixture to make ice pops.

Sugar *and water*

It's best to keep your lemonade in a bottle in the fridge.

Gently pour through a funnel.

Hold on tightly to the bottle.

4 Pour the mixture into a strainer.

5 Let the juice drain through by pressing the mixture with the back of a spoon.

6 Add sugar to taste and the remaining water.

7 Bottle your lemonade.

Shark attack

Grrrrrrrr

Let's move it!

Go, go, go!

What's the science?

So, what's floating your boat? The answer is **buoyancy**. Any object placed in water has two forces acting on it: its weight pulling it down and upthrust from the water pushing it up. If the object's weight is too much for the water to support, the object will **sink**. If it's lighter, the object will **float**. The two bottles on your boat are full of air, which is very light. Try filling them with sand or rice and see whether or not they still float.

Weight

Buoyancy

10

Keep your cool

What floats and what doesn't? It's a matter of life and death if there are vicious sharks in the water. Quick, get this boat out of here!

Crafty boats

Think, or you'll sink! All you need to remember is, if it floats it'll make a boat. You'll need it to float if there are sharks around!

You will need:

Use anything you can find that floats for boat-building materials.

To make a basic boat

All you need is a plastic food tray, two plastic bottles, scissors, and string. When you have finished, add special features, such as a control deck or a go-faster spoiler.

Carefully make a hole in each corner, using scissors.

Plastic bottle

Plastic food tray

Plastic bottle

Scissors and string

Tie a piece of string through each hole and around each bottle tightly.

! **Ask an adult** to help when you are near water.

11

Blowing bubbles

Bubbles are out of this world.
These shimmering spheres wobble
into existence, float gently into the air,
then disappear without a trace.
That really is magic!

You will need:
- Dishwashing liquid
- Water • A large bowl
- Wire • Anything with holes in it!

Bubble recipe
Use one large cup of dishwashing liquid, then mix in two large pitchers of water.

Mix the recipe in a big bowl.

What makes a good bubble?

Bend wire or old coat hangers into shapes to make your own blowers.

Blowing bubbles

Make your own bubble mixture, then search your house for things that you think you could blow bubbles through. You can make lots and lots of tiny bubbles or huge giant ones.

See what happens with a draining spoon or strainer.

Close-up of a bubble

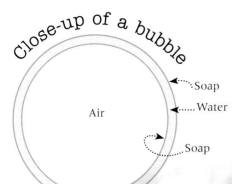

Air

Soap

Water

Soap

What is a bubble?

A bubble is just like a sandwich. Its skin has an inner and outer layer of soap with a thin layer of water in the middle.

Try blowing bubbles with your hands.

Rainbow of colors!

Putting some thin cloth over a tube makes a cloud of froth.

What's the science?
- -

Bubbles only last as long as it takes the water to dry out, and then they go pop. If you poke them, the water escapes much faster. If you blow bubbles on a hot day, they won't last long. On a cold day they will hang around longer and float much higher because your warm breath is lighter than cold air. In icy weather the bubbles may even freeze!

Domino run

On your mark, for a spectacular rush of excitement that ends in an almighty mess. The run takes time to set up, but is thrilling to watch.

Start from a high point, such as a stool or box.

You will need:

- Scissors
- Cardboard tubes
- Tape
- Dominos
- Toys

Tunnels and ramps can be made from cardboard tubes, either whole or cut in half.

It's a complete mess!

You can even make the run go up steps, if they aren't too high.

Away it goes!

The car hits the dominoes, the dominoes ram the car, and whoosh! It flies through the tunnel, straight into the people standing at the bottom!

What's the science?

How can one push knock over all those dominoes? It's all because of moving **energy**. If no energy is being given off and the item is perfectly still we say it has **stored energy**.

When you push the first car you give it some energy. As the car moves, its stored energy is turned into **moving energy** and it falls toward the first domino. When the car hits the domino, that too starts to fall and it hits the next domino. This happens all the way along the chain, until the last object has fallen over. Then you've got to use some energy to clean up the mess!

Chain reaction

Everything is all over the place—as one goes, the others follow. What a mess, and what a noise!

The grand finale

The dominoes crash into the truck, which rolls down the ramp, knocks into the tube carrying the strainer full of candy, which falls and the dinosaur gets his meal. Phew!

Crash, and it's over!

15

Swirling snowstorm

Shake up a storm using just a screw-top jar, water, glycerine, glitter, and a few toys. Add them together, and you'll have the perfect gift for all the movers and shakers you know!

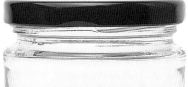

Take a jar

Choose a small jar with a very tight, screw-top lid. You may want to test it— you don't want your snowstorms to leak everywhere.

You will need:
- Jar • Glycerine • Glitter
- Water • Pencil
- Strong glue • Plastic toy

1 Add glitter to glycerine.

2 Fill the jar to the top with water.

3 Stir well.

No **great shakes,** they're easy to make

Glue tip
Use a strong glue that seals even when in water to glue down the toy. For an extra seal, add some glue inside the rim of the lid to prevent leakage.

Glue around the inside of the lid and the outside of the jar rim.

Decorate the lid with festive ribbon.

What's the science?

Watch how the glitter in your snowstorm falls to the bottom of the jar. This happens because of **a force called gravity**, which **acts on everything in the universe.**

On Earth, gravity pulls everything toward the center of the planet. This is extremely useful because it keeps things from flying off into space. No matter how many times you shake your snowstorm, **the glitter feels the pull of gravity** and settles when the water stops moving.

Glycerine
Glycerine is a nontoxic liquid that can be bought in most supermarkets. It thickens the water so that your glitter-snow falls more slowly when you shake the snow globe. Use about one part glycerine to two parts water.

4 Glue down a toy and leave to dry.

5 Screw the lid on tightly.

6 Shake it up!

Ice lantern

Light up the night with shining ice decorations and glowing ice lanterns. You can use any seasonal leaves and flowers to decorate your creations—just get outside, start picking, and create a welcoming light in your yard.

The big freeze

Position a small bowl inside a larger one and tape it so that it is hanging in the center—not touching the bottom or sides. Fill it with foliage and water, and freeze it.

Defrost tip

To remove the bowls, dip the frozen lantern in warm water and pour a little into the smaller bowl as well, to loosen the ice.

If the small bowl bobs up too much, put some pebbles in it to weigh it down.

You will need:

- Large and small bowls • Natural materials like leaves and flowers • Water • Tape • Candles • Lids or trays • String

Frosty glow

Use half a plastic bottle and a cup for the long lanterns, making sure that the cup doesn't touch the edges of the bottle at all. Use small or tall candles for the inside and if it starts to defrost, perk it up by putting it back into the freezer for a while.

You will need:

- Plastic bottle
- Plastic cup
- Tape
- Natural materials like leaves and flowers
- Candles • Water

❗ Ask an adult to light the candles.

1 Fix the containers so that the cup is in the center of the bottle.

2 Arrange the plants in the gap between the cup and the bottle.

Ice art

Find some lids or trays with at least a ½ in (1 cm) tall rim and fill them with water. Put some plant material into the lid, then drape the ends of a long piece of string into the water—they will freeze inside the ice. Hang them outside on trees or bushes.

Tape the string to the sides of the lid to stop it from moving while the water freezes.

What's the science?

Ice is the solid form of water. When the temperature goes down to −32°F (0°C) water starts to freeze and harden. It forms a hard crystal called ice. You may find that your fingers stick to your lantern as you try to get it out of the bowls. This is because the **moisture that is naturally on your hands begins to freeze onto the ice,** gluing your fingers against it. A little warm water will unstick them.

If you are turning out your lantern in a warm room, **the ice may be slippery.** This is because some of the water molecules on the surface of the ice are turning back into a liquid. This thin layer of water makes the ice difficult to grip. **As more of the ice melts, it becomes slipperier.**

3 Fill the gap with water, taking care not to disturb the plant material.

4 Freeze the bottle for several hours. Remove the bottle and the cup.

5 Place a tealight or candle inside the ice.

Grass people

2. Tie a knot in one end and turn the hose inside out.

5. Pinch out a nose and tie it with a rubber band.

6. Soak the head in a bowl of water until it is completely wet through.

1. Cut out a 12 in (30 cm) strip from some nylon hose.

3. Place a handful of grass seed inside.

4. Fill the rest of the bag with sawdust and tie a knot in the top.

Keep your hair on!

Once you have prepared your head, put it upright in a dish. Make sure the nose is in the right place—remember, grass always grows upward. Sprinkle it with water every day, and when the hair has gone wild, give it a haircut.

You will need:

- Scissors • Hose
- Grass seeds
- Sawdust
- Rubber band
- Gravel • Plant pot
- Soil

The grass seeds are now at the top. .....

Give it a face. Stick on eyes and other features. .....

Bad hair day?

Grow the grass in a pot instead. Sow the seeds and in a few weeks the grassy hair sprouts and grows. But if you don't take control, it will grow and grow and grow!

Grow these anytime

Planting time

Place some gravel at the bottom of the pot, fill it with soil, and sprinkle a handful of seeds on the surface. Keep the soil damp and place the pot in a warm, light place, and whatever you do, don't let the plant grow out of control!

What's the science?

There are thousands of different types of grass, many of which we use as **food**—wheat, rice, and corn are all edible grasses. Animals eat grasses, too. Luckily, the **growing point** of the grass is at the base of the blade, so animals can grab a mouthful without damaging the plant, which quickly regrows. So remember, however many times you cut your plant's hair, it will grow back again!

Roots and shoots

Roots go down and shoots go up.
Let's see if beans know which way to grow.

Try these any time of year

Which beans can you try?

Butter   Kidney   Cannellini   Black-eyed   Navy   Soy   Aduki

Bean machines

Place a selection of dried beans in a glass, fill the glass with water, and soak them overnight. Prepare another glass with damp paper towels wrapped around the inside. When your beans have finished soaking, carefully place them around the edge.

You will need:
- Dried beans
- A glass
- Paper towels

Make sure you cover the beans in water when you soak them.

Who won the race? Which bean is the fastest?

The bean skin is still hanging on.

The race is on!

After about two days the beans will begin to sprout. Do the roots go down and shoots go up? What happens if you turn the beans upside down? Remember to keep them moist.

Keep the paper moist.

Mixed beans

Mung beans

Mustard seeds

Cress seeds

Scatter the **seeds** and grow a **field!**

A good crop

Try your hand at growing wheat grains. These grains came from a local farm. The seed grows into wheat and then produces grain, which is used to make bread. You could grow whole wheat, rye, or barley. Soak the grains overnight in a glass and then simply lay them on damp paper towels. Keep the paper towels moist and watch your wheat field grow.

Soak the grains overnight before laying them on damp paper towels.

Check daily that the paper is moist.

What's the science?

Plants always know which way is up. How do they do this? **Roots and shoots** each have a job to do, so they figure out which way to grow to get what they need. **Plants need water and nutrients from soil.** The tiny roots respond to the pull of gravity by growing down toward the center of the Earth, digging themselves into the soil. **Shoots need light and air to make food.** They sense the warmth of the sun above them, so they grow toward the light.

Sweet tomatoes

Tiny tomatoes. Big taste! Look for small varieties, such as cherry tomatoes. They not only taste the sweetest, but the plants also grow only to about 16 in (40 cm) high. This allows you to grow them in small pots, and you won't need stakes to support them.

You will need:
- Small and large pots
- Tomato seeds
- Compost
- Plant food

The tiny, sweet tomatoes are the best for tasty, bite-size snacks.

Growing a plant

1 Fill a small pot with compost. Push a seed into the center, just below the soil.

2 Place the pot on a windowsill and give is some water. Check it every day to make sure the soil is moist. In about a week, the seed should sprout.

3 When the plant has outgrown the pot, gently move it to a bigger one.

4 Feed the plant with plant food, water it regularly, and wait for flowers to appear.

Cover the seed with compost.

At two weeks

At four weeks

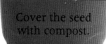

Keep me fed and watered

Tomato tips

Planting seeds

Cut open a tomato and scoop out the seeds. Dry them with paper towels, then plant them instead of store-bought seeds. What do you think will happen?

Packet of tomato seeds.

Ladybug friends

If you see a ladybug on your tomato plant, don't move it. Ladybugs are your friends. They eat the greenflies that want a bite of your tomatoes.

Tomato snacks

Wait until the tomatoes are fully red, then pick them and eat them as snacks. You will find that your homegrown tomatoes are tastier than store-bought ones.

When you see flowers, you'll know the fruit is on its way. The flowers disappear and the baby tomatoes grow in their place. After a few weeks, the fruit will ripen.

Start sowing seeds in early spring.

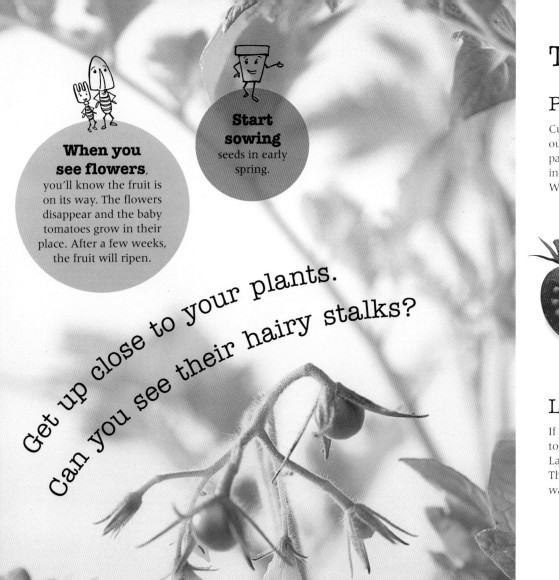

Get up close to your plants. Can you see their hairy stalks?

What's the science?

If you brush the **hairs on a tomato stem** you will notice that they are slightly sticky. There is a reason for this—**they are used to trap insects**. An insect gets stuck and dies, then wind, rain, or gravity dumps the insect onto the ground under the plant. Its body slowly breaks down to provide nutrients for the plant roots. Quite a lot of insects can be caught in this way. Potato plants, which are relatives of the tomato, do it, too.

Senses garden

Scratch and sniff your way around some deliciously smelly plants.

You will need:

- Plants
- Plant pots
- Small stones
- Soil

Self-contained herb garden

Conjure up an instant herb garden in a pot. Choose herbs for their smell, color, or taste. Decorate the container with a design that suits your pot garden. Keep it watered and in a warm, sheltered spot.

1 Pick four or five small plants.

Chives

2 Place small stones in the pot for drainage.

Decorate a plant pot

3 Add the plants and fill with soil.

Touchy-feely

The more you touch herbs, the more they give off their smell. Rub the leaves between your fingers and smell them.

Touch

Good scents

Every herb plant has its own special smell. Some are sweet and some are sharp. Can you identify a herb just from its smell?

Soft and furry

Crisp and curly

Sound

Stop! Listen

If your plants are outside, stop and listen for a moment. Can you hear buzzing? Bees love the fragrant flowers of herbs like thyme, lemon balm, and rosemary.

Look out

Decorate your garden with painted pots and plant labels to show what's growing where.

Sight

............These plant labels are made from ping-pong balls on sticks.

Taste

Good taste

Herbs can help to make food taste even better. Chop up the leaves or use them whole.

Water your plants regularly.

What's the science?

Herbs and many other plants, such as onions and garlic, have a particular smell. There are two reasons for this. **Some plants need to attract insects** to their flowers so that they can produce seeds to make new plants. In others, the **smell** and **taste** are there to **stop animals from eating them**. This prevents the plant from being damaged, so it can survive and grow bigger.

...Dried catnip

Catnip sock

Create a face on a colorful sock with buttons and beads, then fill the sock with catnip. Add rice or dried peas to make it heavier. Tie a knot and let your cat loose on it.

Smell

Marjoram

Look at all the plant colors and shapes. Silver, purple, orange, green. Feathery, wispy, furry, wrinkly.

Apple mint

Parsley

Sage

Lemon balm

Paper weaving

Under, over, under, over. Don't throw paper away—turn it into art. Weave pictures and turn them into cards, or stick them on the wall.

You will need:

- Envelope
- Paper
- Scissors

1 Take an envelope and cut along the short sides and one long side. Cut off the flap, too.

2 When you open it out you should have a large sheet of paper, like this.

Cut wiggly lines up the sheet for a wavy look.

Cut lots of paper strips that fit across the width of the sheet.

3 Fold the paper in half again and draw evenly spaced lines down the sheet.

4 Cut the strips from the folded edge but STOP before you get to the top.

5 Open the sheet out and start weaving—under, over, under, over—until you reach the end. Remember to start the next strip in the opposite way—over, under, over, under.

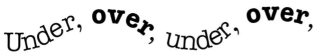
Picture weave

You can use a picture from a magazine as your backing sheet, then weave plain strips along it.

Weave art

Experiment with your weaving by using pictures or patterns as well as plain paper. Use any paper you can find.

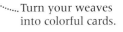

.....Turn your weaves into colorful cards.

Try patterned strips and a plain background.

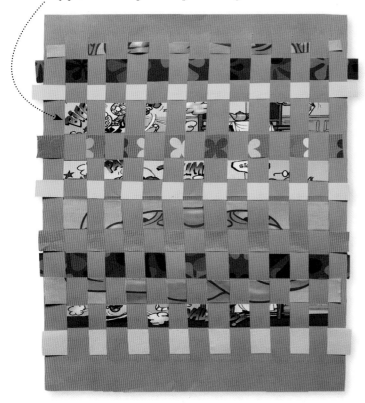

What's the science?

A thin strip of paper is reasonably **strong along its length**, but it is too narrow to hold or balance anything on. However, if you interlace strips under and over **at right angles** to each other, they create a piece of paper that is strong yet still **flexible**. This is because the strength in the length of the strip is now going across as well as up and down. A fabric loom uses the same idea by weaving strands of fabric together to create cloth.

29

Casting shadows

shadows

You will need:

• A camera—a cheap disposable or a phone
• Some willing models
• Your imagination
• Lots of bright sunshine

View the world from some strange angles using shadows made by the sun, and then capture them on camera.

What's the science?

- - - - - - - - - - - - -

Shadows occur when an object **blocks the path of light rays**. The amount of light that is blocked depends on whether the object is **solid** or **transparent** (see-through). Solid objects cast the strongest shadows because most of the light rays are reflected back from the object's surface, creating a dark shadow. Transparent items, such as glass bottles, let almost all the light through. They still cast a blurry shadow, mainly around the edges of the object.

Call me Turkey!

Special effects

Hand shadows against a wall are great, but why not use your whole body to create some really strange shadow effects? You could even base a story around your shadow photos.

Invisible ink

Want to keep something secret? Here's a way to stop your plans from falling into enemy hands. You don't need fancy spy equipment—all you need is a lemon!

Now you see it...

You will need:
- Lemon • Bowl
- Paintbrush or cotton swabs • Paper
- An Iron

Lemons can do magic!

Making ink

1 Squeeze a lemon into a bowl.

Draw quickly, so you can check your work before it dries.

2 Write your secret message on the paper in lemon juice using a paintbrush or cotton swab.

3 To decipher the message, ask someone to iron the paper with a hot iron until the message comes through.

Book of magic

Keep your tricks and spells safe and sound in your very own magic book. Take two pieces of cardboard and some paper, punch two holes down one side of them, and tie them together with a ribbon.

Tear the edges of the paper for an aged effect.

These magic messages will remain invisible to all non-wizards

Glue your spells into your magic book.

Rub a damp tea bag over your paper to make it look old.

! Ask an adult to help you with the iron—it gets hot!

What's the science?

This trick works because **lemon juice is an acid**. When you put it on the paper the **acid destroys some of the paper surface**, so that when you heat it, the areas with the message turn brown first. If you don't have lemon juice, you can also use milk, which is slightly acidic.

Baffling balloons

Everyone knows that balloons pop if you stick something sharp into them. Show off your magical talents by skewering a balloon without it going BANG!

Non-pop balloon

All you need for this amazing trick is some tape. Simply stick a piece on the balloon and, miraculously, you can poke a sharp stick or pin carefully through the tape. Prepare your balloon with tape before you perform your trick.

Stick on a strip of tape about ½ in (2 cm) long.

Don't inflate the balloon too much.

You will need:

- Long toothpick or a pin • Clear tape
- Scissors • Balloon

What's the science?

Why doesn't the balloon **pop** when you skewer it? Balloons are made of stretchy **rubber**. As you **blow** into a balloon the rubber **molecules** are **forced apart**, especially around the widest part of the balloon, making it less strong. If you put a pin into it, a **rip** races around the surface of the balloon where the molecules are most **stretched**. Placing the tape on it stops that rip from happening.

Increased pressure at the edge of the tear makes the rip spread.

Be **bold**, stick it through!

Will it go **POP?**

Skewered balloon

The secret of this trick is to prepare the balloon before you show anyone. Once all of the skewers are in place you won't fail to amaze. Practice removing the balloon from the tube at the end of the trick without showing that it is twisted.

This tube is 5 x 3 in (13 x 8 cm). ......

❗ **Ask an adult** to make the holes with something sharp.

1 Poke pairs of holes through opposite sides of the tube—look at the box (bottom) to see where you should make them.

Add some decoration

2 Paint the tube silver, to make it look like metal, and decorate it.

Give it a **twist** and slip on the tube

Add some decoration to your tube.

2 Blow up a long balloon, but not too much, or you will not be able to twist it. Twist the balloon in the middle and cover the twist with the tube.

What? No pop?

3 Push the skewers through, avoiding the twisted center. You may have to push back the balloon with your thumb to help get the skewers through.

4 To perform the trick, set up the balloon with the skewers before you start your baffling performance. Pull the skewers out slowly, one at a time. Secretly untwist the balloon as you remove it from the tube.

What's the secret?

Twist the balloon in the middle to keep it from being skewered. But don't tell anyone!

Don't pull the skewers out too fast or the balloon may pop.

Place holes so the skewers miss the middle. ...

Make sure the twist is in the gap in the middle before you put the skewers in.

Mirac

Amaze an audier
balancing your pet bu
on the tips of pencils,
or even your nos
float as if by M

They can float anywhere— make lots and lots!

Attach weight here.

Use glue to stick a small coin or washer to both wing tips.

Fly template

Use this outline to make your floating pet butterfly.

- Fold a piece of tracing paper in half and draw around the dotted line.
- Cut out this wing shape and open out the tracing paper.
- Trace the whole shape onto a piece of thin cardboard.

Fold the tracing paper here

Doing the trick

To ensure that the audience is completely confused, hand everyone a butterfly without the weights attached. They'll be baffled when they can only balance it in the middle of its body!

Use thin cardboard, such as a cereal box.

Make sure

both sides are exactly the same.

butterflies

Don't tell anyone the secret!

What's the science?

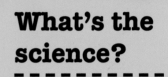

The butterfly balances through its **center of gravity**. This is the spot where the weight on one side is the same as the weight on the other. When there are no weights attached to the butterfly, its center of gravity is in the middle of its body. When the weights are attached, **the center of gravity shifts up toward the butterfly's head**. Once it has stabilized around its new center of gravity, the butterfly balances quite happily on its nose.

Try it out on your fingertips

2 Color it in.

3 Glue the weights onto the underside of the cardboard.

Powerful Potions

Believe it or not, there are magic ingredients in your very own kitchen. You just need to know which ones to mix together to get the explosive results!

! Ask an adult

All of the ingredients are completely safe, but most of the mixtures taste really yucky. So don't drink them unless you are told you can by an adult.

You will need:

- Baking soda
- Salt • Vinegar
- Food coloring
- Carbonated drink

Croak, Croak!

What's the science?

When you open a bottle of soda you hear a **whooshing** sound. This is the sound of **carbon dioxide gas** escaping. The gas is what makes the drink fizzy. At the factory, **the gas is forced into the drink under high pressure**, which makes it dissolve in the liquid. When you release the lid, the **carbon dioxide slowly escapes from the liquid by forming bubbles.** Adding salt makes bubbles form faster, because the crystals have a rough surface that allows more bubbles to grow on them. The bubbles all rush to the top of the liquid together, making the froth overflow.

Bubble and fizz

For an instant fizz, simply fill a small glass with any kind of carbonated drink you like. Then all you have to do is pour a teaspoon of salt on top. Add some food coloring for multicolored bubbles.

Pour salt into the drink

Watch it fizz all over

Instant inflation

Amaze an audience by telling them that you will blow up a balloon without blowing at all.

First, pour some vinegar into a bottle.

Next, pour a teaspoon of baking soda into a balloon and stretch it over the bottle's neck.

Don't let the soda out yet!

Pick up the balloon and empty out the baking soda.

Add the secret ingredient... release the magic!

As the baking soda mixes with the vinegar it creates bubbles of carbon dioxide gas that escape into the balloon, making it blow up by itself. Let's hope it doesn't explode!

It has blown up by itself— no one has touched it

Look! It's still growing. When will it stop?

Magic folds

How can you turn a flat, flimsy piece of paper into a strong box? Can you make paper fly? Try your hand at some paper-folding magic.

You will need:

- Lots of paper
- Stapler

You can use newspaper, comics, or colored paper.

Try different paper sizes for big or small boxes.

What's the science?

Try folding a sheet of paper in half as many times as you can. How many times can you manage? No matter how hard you try, you can probably only fold it six or seven times. This is because **every time you fold the paper it becomes twice as thick**. Eventually, the paper has too small an area and is too thick to bend without a lot of effort. The record stands at 13 folds, using a very long piece of paper.

Perform PAPER magic

Fold and hold—just a few folds and tucks, and a flat piece of paper becomes a sturdy box. That's paper magic!

1 Fold a rectangle of paper in half and half again four times to make 16 squares. Then unfold it.

2 Bring the top and bottom flaps into the center.

3 Fold each corner down two-thirds to the center.

4 Fold the central edges of the paper level with the corners.

5 Turn the edges of the paper back to make flaps.

6 Hold the center of the two sides and pull them apart.

7 Pinch each corner from top to bottom to help form the shape of the box.

Open up!

8

9 Cut a wide strip of paper for a handle.

Staple the handle to each side.

Try out patterned paper or paint a piece yourself.

Watch paper fly!

Make a paper plane—a few simple folds and it flies!

1 Take a rectangle of paper and fold it in half.

2 Turn down one corner, as shown.

3 Fold the same corner down again.

4 Now fold the top part down to make a wing.

5 Make the other wing.

6 Repeat the folds on the other half of the paper.

7 Open out the wings, turn the plane over, and whiz it across the room!

Mysterious metal

Some metals are attracted to magnets—that's the magic of metal—so dig out those magnets. Here's how to make metal work for you.

You will need:

- Magnets • Paper clips
- Cans • Toys • Jar lids
- Glue • Cardboard
- Paper fastener
- Scissors

Test your metal

Find out whether metals are magnetic by touching a magnet onto various objects—if it sticks, they're magnetic.

Fishing game

Cut fish shapes out of thin cardboard and fasten a paper clip or paper fastener onto them. Tie a magnet onto a piece of string, tie the string to a pencil, then race your friends to pick up the fish.

Tidy tins

Tin cans are great to reuse as storage. Because they are metal, you can decorate them with magnets. You can even spell out what is in them with letter magnets.

❗ Ask an adult to cut the top off the can. Make sure it's clean and free of sharp edges.

Homemade fridge magnets

Glue a magnet to the top of a jar or bottle lid, then glue a small toy to the other side. Stick your magnets onto tins or even the fridge door.

Small toys

Magnets

Reuse lids from jars

Glue

Make a moving picture

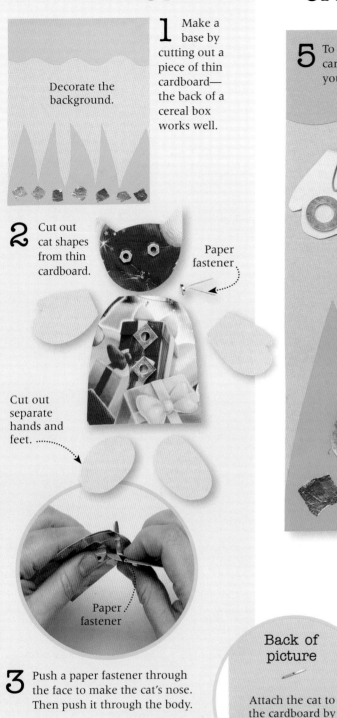

1 Make a base by cutting out a piece of thin cardboard—the back of a cereal box works well.

Decorate the background.

2 Cut out cat shapes from thin cardboard.

Paper fastener

Cut out separate hands and feet.

Paper fastener

3 Push a paper fastener through the face to make the cat's nose. Then push it through the body.

Back of picture

Attach the cat to the cardboard by pressing the paper fastener through the back.

4 Now make four chains of four paper clips each. Attach these to the cat's hands and feet, then to its body.

Crazy cat—make him dance!

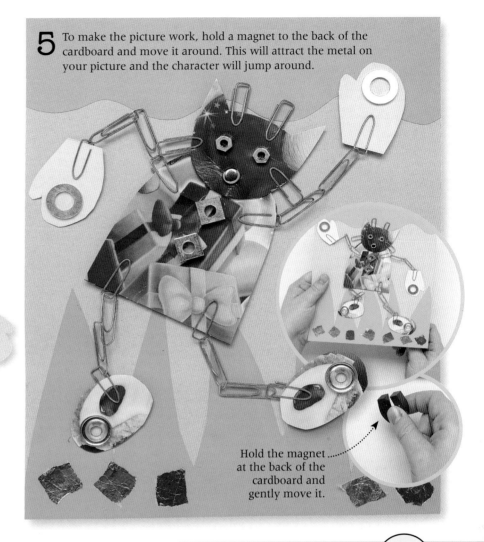

5 To make the picture work, hold a magnet to the back of the cardboard and move it around. This will attract the metal on your picture and the character will jump around.

Hold the magnet at the back of the cardboard and gently move it.

What's the science?

Magnets are special metals that can create an **invisible force field** around themselves. This force is strong enough to attract other magnetic objects to them. The way the force flows around the magnet creates a **"pole"** at each end. Each pole attracts its opposite pole. Magnetic metals have poles as well, so the poles on the metal will be attracted to the opposite poles on the magnet and they will stick firmly together.

North pole

Force field

N

S

South pole

Marbled paper

Create mind-boggling effects on paper without a paintbrush—you'll be amazed! You can use your paper to wrap presents or you can fold it into origami shapes.

Ask an adult to help mix the paint with turpentine.

The paint mixture

Before you start, make some pots of paint mixture in different colors. Squeeze a blob of oil paint into a pot and add four capfuls of turpentine. Mix them together. The paint will become very thin.

Paper towels

Spoon

White paper

Paint pots

Toothpick

Turpentine

Baking pan with water

Oil paints

3 Float the paper on the surface and gently push it down to help it make contact.

4 Pick up the corners and quickly lift out the paper.

1 Pour about 1 in (3 cm) of water into the pan. Add small spoonfuls of each paint color.

2 With a toothpick, swirl the paint gently in the water, but don't mix it too much.

5 Leave the paper to dry flat on a thick layer of newspaper.

What's the science?

Oil and water don't mix, which is why the paint floats on top of the water. This happens because **water molecules are tightly packed together**, making the water more dense (thick) so that it sinks to the bottom. The oil molecules are not as closely packed as the water so they float on top. **Oil doesn't dissolve in water** so even if you whisk the two together they will eventually separate into two layers.

Oil molecules

Water molecules

Oil

Water

Whole grain bread

Make bread taste more interesting by using grainy flour and sprinklings of seeds inside and out. Granary bread is fun to bake and eat.

You will need:

Butter
2 tbsp

Granary bread flour
1¾ cups

White
bread flour
1¾ cups

1 sachet
fast-acting yeast
(2 teaspoons)

1 teaspoon brown sugar
1 teaspoon salt

Warm water
1¼ cups

A beaten
egg for
a glossy
finish

Bread tips

Yeast needs warmth to help it grow. Follow these tips to ensure that your bread rises.
• If all the things you work with are warm, such as the bowl and the room, this will help.
• Make sure the water isn't too hot. Hot water will kill the yeast and your bread won't rise.

Makes 12
rolls

Equipment:

• Mixing bowl
• Knife
• Wooden spoon
• Plastic wrap
• Baking sheet
• Pastry brush
• Cooling rack

What's the science?

One of the ingredients in dough is yeast. **Yeast is a living thing—it is a type of fungus** and is related to mushrooms and molds. Bakers add yeast to bread because it feeds on the sugars in flour and **produces bubbles of carbon dioxide gas**. This gas makes the dough expand to double its size. Cooking traps the gas as the dough hardens in the heat, leaving you with a light, spongy texture to your bread.

1 Put the flours, yeast, sugar, and salt in a bowl and rub in the butter until the mixture looks like bread crumbs.

Roll it into a ball with your hands.

Mix it up

2 Make a well and pour in the water. Add some seeds now; set some aside to sprinkle on top.

3 Mix with a wooden spoon until the dough comes away from the bowl.

Knead the dough

4 Sprinkle some flour on the work surface. Stretch the dough and fold it over.

What's the science?

Flour contains **a protein called gluten**. Kneading the dough makes the gluten soft and stretchy so that it can **trap the bubbles of carbon dioxide gas being produced by the yeast**. Without kneading, the dough goes flat because the gas bubbles escape.

Keep kneading

5 Press your knuckles into the dough. Add more flour if needed. Repeat steps 4 and 5 for 6 minutes.

Divide it up

6 Make into a ball and cut it into 12 even-sized pieces. Roll them into small balls and place on a greased baking sheet.

7 Cover with plastic wrap and leave in a warm place for about 40 minutes to rise. Preheat the oven to 425°F (220°C).

8 When the rolls have doubled in size, they are ready to decorate. Brush them with beaten egg. Now sprinkle the seeds over the top.

9 Bake for 20 to 25 minutes. Remove the rolls from the oven and cool on a rack.

⚠️ **Ask an adult** to help with the oven.

Get ready to eat!

Sesame seeds

Poppy seeds

You will need:
• Lots of different seeds

Sunflower seeds

Pumpkin seeds

49

Popcorn

Have a Pop at making Popcorn. But keep the lid on, or it'll Pop everywhere!

Pop Pop Pop Pop Pop Pop

Sweet or salty

Sprinkle sugar or salt over your popcorn while it is still in the pan.

What's the science?

What makes a kernel of corn explode when you heat it? Well, inside every kernel is a mixture of **oil, water, protein,** and **starch.** When you heat the kernels, the **water tries to turn into steam** but is held in by the kernel's tough outer skin. The rest of the seed turns into a paste. When the seed case can't contain the steam any more, it splits apart. The steam is released so fast **it blows the paste into a foam, which cools and sets.**

Pop*

*Pop *Pop

Cook for about a minute, or until there are no more pops.

⓪ Ask an adult to help with the very hot pan.

1 Heat the oil. Let it get really hot before you add the corn kernels.

2 Put on the lid, then listen for pops. When the kernels stop popping, gentle shake the pan.

You won't need any heat under the pan.

3 Turn off the heat and take a peek. Take the pan off the stove to cool.

4 Stir in the butter and your popcorn is ready to eat.

Bags of flavor
For more exciting tastes to add to your buttered popcorn:
1. Pour your popcorn into a clean plastic bag.
2. Shake in grated cheese or dried herbs.
3. Squeeze the top of the bag, shake it around, then serve.

You will need:

Self-rising flour
1 cup

Butter (room temperature)
8 tbsp

Sugar
⅔ cup

2 eggs

1 tsp
baking powder

1 tsp
vanilla
extract

Makes 24
cupcakes

Equipment:

- Mixing bowl
- Electric mixer
- 2 cupcake pans
- Baking cups
- Cooling rack
- Strainer

Conjure some fairy cupcakes

What's the science?

The secret to making good cupcakes is to make lots of **bubbles** and hold them in the mixture. **Beating** the ingredients adds air bubbles to the mix. **Baking powder** produces more bubbles when it mixes with the wet egg. All the bubbles become trapped in the sticky, stretchy batter formed by the flour and eggs. As the cupcakes bake, the mixture hardens around the bubbles and turns into a spongy solid.

There is a lot of science in a cake. Baking is all about chemistry and how the ingredients combine. You have to get everything just right for a cake that is light, fluffy, and scrumptious.

Preheat the oven
to 375°F (190°C).

1 Sift the flour and baking powder. Sifting adds air and gets rid of lumps.

Add everything else

2 Beat the eggs and add them with the butter, sugar, and vanilla extract to the flour.

Beat until it's creamy. Does it drop off a spoon?

3 If the batter drops off easily in a dollop, then it's ready.

Fill up the cups

4 Put a teaspoon of batter in each baking cup. Bake in the oven for 20 minutes.

5 Take out of the oven when golden brown.

6 Leave to cool. Now decorate!

54

Rainbow icing

Mix up lots of little bowls of different colored icing. For green icing, blend yellow and blue; for orange, mix yellow and red. Use anything sweet to decorate the tops, such as candied cherries, raisins, candies, etc.

You will need:

- 1 tbsp confectioners' sugar • 1 tsp water
- 1 drop food coloring
- Candies
- Writing icing

To ice 4 cupcakes:

1 Combine the confectioners' sugar, water, and food coloring.

2 Drop a dollop of icing into the center of the cupcake and let it spread.

Cherry

3 Decorate it with anything sweet. Use tubes of writing icing for extra patterns.

What's the science?

Baking the cupcakes sets all the ingredients. First, it makes the **bubbles expand** and double in size. As the heat increases, the **egg and flour proteins begin to harden**. The tops and edges of the cupcakes turn brown as the sugar caramelizes. The **temperature is crucial**: if the oven is too cool, the gas bubbles escape before the mixture sets, leaving flat, heavy cupcakes. If it is too hot, then the outsides bake before the middle, producing cracked, peaked cupcakes.

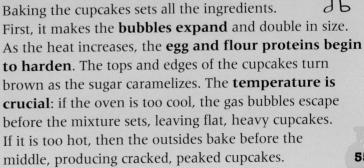

It's ready when you can turn the bowl upside down over your head without the whites sliding out.

Use a big clean bowl.

Use the mixer at top speed.

3 Keep beating until the whites are stiff and form trails around the beaters.

1 Separate the white of the egg from the yolk. Pour into a bowl.

2 The whites turn frothy as you beat them.

Meringue mountains

Build your own mountain range using nothing but eggs and sugar. Pile up your cooked meringues to make a snowy mountain peak that looks good and is delicious to eat.

Grease the sheet, then cover with parchment paper.

! **Preheat** the oven to 275°F (140°C).

7 Spoon out the mixture and swirl it to form soft peaks.

! **Bake** in the oven for 2 hours.

8 After baking, let sit for a few hours to dry out.

4 Add the sugar one tablespoon at a time while beating. Repeat until all the sugar is used up.

Use a lower speed to mix in the sugar.

5 When all the sugar is in, beat the mixture one last time.

Mixture should stand up in firm points.

6 Now it's ready. The mixture should look smooth and glossy.

You will need:

Sugar ⅔ cup

2 large egg whites

Electric mixer

Mixing bowl

Teaspoon

Soup spoon

Parchment paper

Baking sheet

Pastry brush

Pile them high!

What's the science?

Getting a crisp meringue from a sloppy egg white involves some effort. Egg whites are a mixture of protein and water. **Beating unravels the protein and creates air bubbles that become trapped, making it foamy.** Adding sugar makes the protein stronger and more elastic. Meringues are cooked at a low temperature to allow the water to evaporate and the protein to set hard around the bubbles.

57

Chocolate chunk cookies

Brown sugar
½ cup

Sugar
⅓ cup

Butter
8 tbsp

1 Egg

All-purpose flour
1⅓ cups

Baking soda
1 teaspoon

Forget store-bought cookies. These are much tastier! Use good quality chocolate, chopped up into big chunks.

☺ Makes 12 cookies

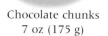

Chocolate chunks
7 oz (175 g)

Equipment

Mixing bowl

Spoon

Knife

Wooden spoon

Pastry brush

Baking sheet

Cooling rack

1 Cream the butter and sugar together until fluffy.

Soft butter is easier to mix with the sugar.

2 Mix in the egg. Ask an adult to preheat the oven to 375°F (190°C).

Add beaten egg

3 Stir in the flour and mix all the ingredients thoroughly.

4 Add the chocolate. Get help chopping it into chunks.

5 Spoon four heaps on the sheet.

Stick some extra chunks on top of the heaps before baking.

6 Bake for 10–12 minutes, then ask an adult to take them out of the oven.

7 Let them cool before moving to a rack. Clean the sheet for the next batch of cookies.

Yum, yum

What's the science?

One of the lovely things about chocolate is the way it melts in your mouth. That is because it **melts at** a temperature that is very close to **body temperature**. It does this because it contains **cocoa butter**, which is a type of fat found in cocoa beans. Dark, milk, and white chocolate all contain different amounts of cocoa butter.

Glossary

Acid

Acids are sharp-tasting or sour substances. Lemon juice, soda, and vinegar are all mild acids.

Atom

Atoms are the invisible building blocks of the universe. They can join together to form molecules that make up most of the things you see around you, and even some of the ones you can't, such as gases.

Baking powder

This is a mixture of chemicals used in baking to make a cake rise. It works by producing carbon dioxide gas bubbles to make a cake light and spongy.

Baking soda

Bicarbonate is one of the ingredients of baking soda. It reacts with an acid to produce carbon dioxide gas.

Buoyancy

The ability of something to float is called its buoyancy. It depends on the weight of the object and how much liquid is underneath pushing it upward.

Carbon dioxide

Carbon dioxide is a colorless, odorless gas. Naturally found in the atmosphere, it is also produced by plants and animals, and by chemical reactions.

Citric acid

This is the acid found in citrus fruits such as lemons and oranges.

Crystal

A crystal is a solid material whose atoms are arranged in a regular pattern. Salt, sugar, and ice are all examples of crystals.

Energy

Energy is the ability of something to do work. This work can take different forms: heat, light, movement, gravity, chemical, and nuclear are just some types of energy. Energy can be converted from one form to another and stored until it is needed.

Floating

Objects float when they have buoyancy. This can happen when the object is placed into a liquid or into the air (if it is light enough). Objects that are too heavy will sink.

Force

A force is usually a push or a pull between two objects. Forces always happen in pairs—when one object exerts a force on another object it experiences a force in return. Forces can make things move, change their speed and direction, or change their shape.

Gluten

Gluten is a protein found in cereals such as wheat, barley, and rye. It is produced during bread making and makes the dough elastic and stretchy, giving the baked bread its spongy texture.

Gravity

Gravity is an invisible force pulling objects toward the center of Earth. It also keeps the planets orbiting the sun.

Herb

A herb is a plant whose leaves, seeds, or flowers can be used for perfume or to flavor food or medicine.

Kneading

This is the process of pulling and stretching a dough to encourage gluten to form faster.

Light ray

A ray is the path that light travels on between two points.

Magnet

A magnet is a piece of iron or other material that can attract another magnetic object to it by the invisible force of magnetism.

Magnetic field

This is the region around a magnet where the magnetic force will work. The field creates a force that can pull two magnets together or push them apart.

Metal

Metal is a solid substance that is hard, usually shiny, and can allow heat or electricity to pass through it. Metals can be bent or pulled into shapes.

Molecule

A molecule is a group of two or more atoms that are joined together by internal bonds. The atoms can all be the same or different.

Moving energy

This is the energy that an object has after a force has been applied to it to make it move. It is also known as kinetic energy.

Nitrogen

Nitrogen is a colorless gas that makes up most of the atmosphere. Its atoms are vital to all living things because they are a key ingredient of proteins.

Nutrients

A nutrient is a substance used by living things so that they can survive, grow, and reproduce.

Pole

A pole is the region of a magnet where the magnetic field is strongest. There are usually two poles, one at each end of the magnet. They are described as the north and south poles. A north pole will attract the south pole of another magnet and stick fast. Two north or south poles put close

together repel each other and cannot be pushed together.

Pressure

This is a physical force that is exerted on or against an object by something that is in contact with it. For example, blowing air into a balloon creates pressure on the rubber of the balloon, causing it to stretch. If the pressure is too great, the balloon will burst.

Protein

Proteins are huge molecules that are vital to all living things. They are essential to the structure and function of cells, tissues, and organs in the body of animals and plants.

Solid

A solid is a hard substance that holds its shape until acted on by a strong force.

Sour

This describes one of the basic taste sensations. Sour things have a sharp, sometimes unpleasant, taste or smell that is the opposite of sweet. Lemons and vinegar are sour.

Starch

Starch is an odorless and tasteless white substance found in plants, especially grains and pototoes. It is used by plants as a source of energy.

Steam

This is water that has turned into a gas after being heated to its boiling point. It is also called water vapor.

Stored energy

Stored (or potential) energy is the energy that an object is said to have when it is not doing any work. If a force is applied to the object, the stored energy will be converted into another form of energy.

Taste bud

A taste bud is one of the tiny lumps on the tongue that allows you to taste sweet, sour, salty, bitter, or savory flavors.

Transparent

Something that is easy to see through, such as clear glass or plastic, is said to be transparent.

Index

Acknowledgements

The publisher would like to thank the
following for their kind permission to
reproduce their photographs:

(Key: a-above; b-below/bottom; c-center;
f-far; l-left; r-right; t-top)

12 iStockphoto.com: akinshin (t/bubbles).
13 iStockphoto.com: wundervisuals (main
image). **31 Getty Images:** Martin Barraud / OJO
Images (tr); Stuart McClymont / The Image
Bank (tl); Robert Stahl / The Image Bank (bl).

All other images © Dorling Kindersley
For further information see: www.dkimages.com

See you
again soon